Martin Luther King, Jr. Day

Dianne M. MacMillan

Reading Consultant:

Michael P. French, Ph.D.,
Bowling Green State University

—Best Holiday Books—

Enslow Publishers, Inc.

40 Industrial Road   PO Box 38
Box 398   Aldershot
Berkeley Heights, NJ 07922   Hants GU12 6BP
USA   UK
http://www.enslow.com

> *For my family*
> *Jim, Jeni, Kathy, and Shannon*

Library of Congress Cataloging-in-Publication Data

MacMillan, Dianne.
    Martin Luther King, Jr. Day / Dianne M. MacMillan.
        p. cm. — (Best Holiday Books)
Includes index.
Summary: Describes the life of Martin Luther King and the origin
and celebration of the holiday in his honor.
    ISBN 0-89490-382-9
    1. Martin Luther King Day—Juvenile literature. 2. King, Martin
Luther, Jr., 1929–1968—Juvenile literature. 3. Afro-Americans—
Biography—Juvenile literature. 4. Baptists—United States—
Clergy—Biography—Juvenile literature. 5. Civil rights workers—
United States—Biography—Juvenile literature. [1. King, Martin
Luther, Jr., 1929–1968. 2. Civil rights workers. 3. Clergy.
4. Afro-Americans—Biography. 5. Martin Luther King Day.]
I. Title. II. Series.
E185.97.K5M25 1992
323'.092—dc20
[B]   91-43097
                                                      CIP
                                                         AC

Printed in the United States of America

10 9 8 7

Illustration credits:
AP/Wide World Photos, pp. 16, 18; Bonnie Rhodes, pp. 8, 11; D.C. Public Library, p.
30; Dianne M. MacMillan, p. 40; Georgia Tourist Division, pp. 6, 35; Jill McCarthy,
p. 39; The King Mural by Don Miller, ©District of Columbia Public Library, 1986, p.
13; Library of Congress, pp. 27, 44; National Archives, pp. 4, 25; UPI/Bettmann, pp.
29, 32, 37; Washington Post; reprinted by permission of the D.C. Public Library, pp.
20, 22.

Photo Researcher: Susan Hormuth

Cover illustration: Charlott Nathan

Contents

Dr. Martin Luther King, Jr. was a great leader who helped change unfair laws.

A Man Who Changed History

January 20, 1986, was an important day. It was the very first Martin Luther King, Jr. Day.

Martin Luther King, Jr. believed everyone should be free to make their own choices. They should be free to work at any job, or attend any school. Everyone should be able to do the same things.

At one time, many laws in our country were unfair to African Americans. Martin Luther King, Jr. spent his life fighting to change those laws. He did not fight with weapons. Instead, he fought with words and ideas. He helped change the history of our country.

Martin's home when he was a young boy in Atlanta, Georgia. The home is on Auburn Street.

Martin Luther King, Jr.'s Early Years

Martin Luther King, Jr. was born on January 15, 1929. He lived in Atlanta, Georgia. His parents called him M.L. His sister Willie Christine was one year older. His younger brother, Alfred Daniel, was called A.D. Martin's father was the minister of the Ebenezer Baptist Church. Everyone called Martin's father Daddy King. Martin's mother, Alberta, played the organ and sang in church.

The church was a big part of Martin's early life. On Sundays he listened to his father speak. He loved big words. He saw how words could make people feel happy or sad. He told his mother that some day he was going to use big words like that.

Martin's best friends lived across the street. They played together every day. But one day the boys' mother told Martin to go home. She said her sons could never play with him again. Martin asked why. She said it was because her sons were white. Martin was black. Martin went home crying.

Martin was told by his white friends' mother to go home. She sent him away because he was black.

8

Martin's mother tried to explain. She said that black people were brought to America from Africa long ago. They were brought to work in the fields as slaves. After the Civil War was fought in our country, the slaves were set free. But many white people still did not want to let black people be free. White people made unfair laws. One law said that black children and white children could not go to the same school. Another said that black people could not eat in restaurants where white people ate. There were parks, bathrooms, and drinking fountains that had signs that said "Whites Only." Martin's mother said these laws kept black people and white people apart or separate. Keeping people apart because of race is called segregation. But then she said, "You are as good as anyone."

Martin Becomes a Young Man

Martin loved books. He learned to read before he started school. He also enjoyed all kinds of sports. Even though he was small, he played hard. Everyone wanted him on their baseball or football teams.

Martin was a good speaker. In high school he won prizes for his speeches. Once Martin gave a speech in another town. It was a long bus trip. Buses were segregated. Black people could not sit near white people. They had to sit in the back rows. White people sat in the front rows. But when the seats for white people became filled, black people had to give them their seats.

After Martin gave his speech, he and his teacher left for home. They sat down on the bus. More white people got on. The bus driver told Martin to give up his seat. Martin refused. The bus driver became angry. He called Martin names. He said he would call the police. Martin's teacher asked Martin to obey the law. Martin and his teacher stood for the ninety-mile trip.

African Americans had to sit in the back rows of buses.

Martin skipped the ninth and twelfth grades. He entered Morehouse College when he was fifteen. He decided to become a minister like his father.

After his years at Morehouse, Martin went to Crozer Theological Seminary in Pennsylvania. He made many friends. He graduated as the best student in his class. Martin won money to study at Boston University.

Martin studied the ideas of many great men. He read about Jesus, Frederick Douglass, and Henry David Thoreau. Then Martin studied the life of Mahatma Gandhi.

Gandhi lived in India in the 1940s. Gandhi fought without weapons for freedom. He did this by refusing to obey unfair laws. Even when put in jail, he would not give in. Gandhi never used strong force or violence. Gandhi called this "nonviolent resistance."

While studying at Boston University, Martin met Coretta Scott. She was studying music. They were both from the South. They both liked books, music, and talking about ideas. Soon they fell in love. In 1953 they were married by Martin's father at Coretta's home in Alabama.

People and places important to Martin in his early years included Morehouse College, Morehouse College President Benjamin Mays, and Mahatma Gandhi.

Dexter Avenue Baptist Church

After receiving his degree from Boston University, Martin was called Dr. King. He was hired as minister of the Dexter Avenue Baptist Church in Montgomery, Alabama.

Soon the Kings' first child was born. They named her Yolanda but called her Yoki. Coretta and Martin were very happy. But their lives changed on December 1, 1955. On that day a black woman named Rosa Parks did a brave thing.

Rosa Parks worked in a Montgomery store. At night she was very tired. On Thursday, December 1, 1955, she climbed on the bus and sank into her seat. The bus made more stops.

More white people got on. The bus driver told Rosa to stand. Rosa refused. She was tired, and it was not fair. The bus driver called the police. Rosa was taken to jail.

By Friday everyone in the black neighborhood knew about Rosa. They were angry at the police. They were angry at the bus company. They wanted the bus company to make changes. Martin and other leaders decided to ask all black people to stop riding the buses. This is called a boycott.

Notices were printed and passed out. They said, "Don't ride the bus to work, to town, to school, or any place Monday, December 5." The notice also said to come to a meeting on Monday night.

No one knew if this plan would work. On Monday morning Coretta and Martin looked out their window. A bus went by. It was empty. Then another rolled by. It was also empty. Martin and Coretta were excited.

When Rosa Parks refused to give up her seat on the bus, she was taken to jail. This action led to the Montgomery bus boycott.

All day long, people walked when they had to go someplace. Some had to walk as far as fourteen miles to get to their jobs. That night more than 4000 people came to the meeting. Dr. King spoke. This was the first time most of them had heard him speak. Dr. King said, "There comes a time when people get tired. We are here this evening to say we are tired of being segregated. . ." Everyone cheered. They voted to continue the boycott until the bus company made changes.

A group was formed to lead the boycott. Dr. King was elected president.

Day after day, people stayed away from the buses. Some days it rained and the weather was cold. Black people walked. Some rode horses. Others shared rides. The buses remained empty. Black people were doing a brave and dangerous thing. Dr. King spoke all over Montgomery. He asked people to stay away from the buses.

One night while giving a speech, Dr. King's house was bombed. Quickly, he rushed home.

He found Coretta and Yoki safe. But the front of his house had been destroyed. The police were there. The yard was filled with friends and neighbors. They were angry at the people who bombed Dr. King's house. They had sticks and broken bottles. They were ready to fight the police.

Dr. King spoke to the angry crowd after his house was bombed.

Dr. King told the crowd, "If you have weapons, take them home. We must love our white brothers. We must meet hate with love." He was telling them what he had learned from Jesus and from Gandhi. He was speaking about nonviolence. The crowd went home. No one was hurt.

Finally, the U.S. Supreme Court, the highest court in our country, said that segregation on city buses was wrong. The bus company changed its rules. Black people could sit anywhere on the bus. They no longer had to give up their seats.

Dr. King was asked to speak all over the country.

A New Group Is Formed

After the Montgomery boycott, Dr. King and other black ministers started the Southern Christian Leadership Conference (SCLC). The aim of this group was to change unfair laws. Dr. King went all over the United States. He told everyone how to fight unfair laws. He said they must be peaceful. If the police took them to jail, they should go quietly. Even if people hurt them, they must not hurt others.

People marched down streets carrying signs about unfair laws. As more people heard Dr. King speak, more people tried his ideas. Black college students sat peacefully at white lunch counters. Black people went to white parks. They used bathrooms and drinking fountains that had "Whites Only" signs. Many were put in jail. Some were beaten. Dr. King himself was taken to jail many times.

This was hard for Dr. King's family. His children would ask why Daddy was in jail. And Coretta would say, "Daddy is helping people."

One Sunday Dr. King told the people of the Dexter Avenue Baptist Church that he had to

After the successful bus boycott, African Americans tried to change other unfair laws. Here, a black girl sits at a white lunch counter.

leave. He was moving away from Montgomery. He needed to spend more time with the SCLC. Its office was in Atlanta. The people were very sad. They all joined hands and sang a hymn. Dr. King looked around the room full of friends. He broke down and cried.

"I Have A Dream"

Martin and Coretta moved to Atlanta. They now had four children—Yolanda, Martin III, Dexter, and Bernice. Dr. King was gone a great deal. But when he was home, it was a happy time. Coretta would cook some of Martin's favorite foods. He liked pork chops, fried chicken, black-eyed peas, and greens.

The children loved playing with their father. He would tickle and tease them. A favorite game was to climb halfway up the stairs. Then they would jump into their father's arms. Coretta was worried that one of them might be hurt. But no one ever was.

The SCLC decided to fight segregation in Birmingham, Alabama. Birmingham was one of the most segregated cities in the South. Dr. King believed that if they could change laws in Birmingham, they would be able to change them in other cities.

In 1963, Dr. King went to Birmingham. He wanted lunch counters, bathrooms, elevators, and drinking fountains in stores to be open to everyone.

The King family enjoyed having dinner together when Dr. King was at home.

Birmingham law said people could not march or have a public meeting. Dr. King started a march with forty people. The police arrested them. The next day more people marched. The police attacked them with clubs and dogs. Fire hoses with powerful streams of water were turned on them. Every day people marched. Every day they were put in jail. Dr. King was sent to jail for eight days.

The children of Birmingham asked to march, too. Some were only six years old. At first Dr. King said no. He was afraid they might be hurt. But then he changed his mind. He said the children were already being hurt by segregation.

On May 2, over 1000 black children marched down the street singing the song "We Shall Overcome." No one thought the children would be attacked. But they were wrong. Water was turned on the children. Then they were attacked. The police arrested 959 boys and girls!

That night people all over the country watched the news. They saw the children. They saw what happened. Many were angry and upset. Finally the men who ran the city met with the black leaders. They ended the unfair laws. Freedom for African Americans had come to Birmingham!

On August 28, 1963, Martin Luther King, Jr. and other black leaders marched into

Dr. King speaks to reporters in Birmingham.

Washington, D.C. They were followed by 250,000 people. Most of the people were black. But there were also thousands of white people. They wanted to join Dr. King's fight for freedom.

The crowd gathered in front of the Lincoln Memorial. There were songs and speeches. Then Dr. Martin Luther King, Jr. spoke. He said, "I have a dream today!" And then he told of his dream:

> I have a dream that one day on the red hills of Georgia, sons of former slaves and sons of former slave-owners will be able to sit down at the table of brotherhood. . . .
>
> I have a dream that my four little children will one day live in a nation where they will not be judged by the color of their skin but by the content of their character.

He dreamed of freedom ringing from every mountain. He dreamed of all God's children joining hands. He dreamed of all men singing together, "We are free at last."

When Dr. King had finished speaking, people cheered. Many were crying. Then everyone joined hands and sang together, "We Shall Overcome."

Dr. King's words inspired the crowds of people at the Lincoln Memorial. He spoke of his dreams for a better world.

Dr. King with Coretta, his parents, sister Willie Christine, and brother A.D. after receiving the Nobel Peace Prize.

The Nobel Peace Prize

Each year the country of Norway gives a prize. The prize goes to the person who has done the most for peace in the world for that year. It is called the Nobel Peace Prize. In October 1964, Martin Luther King, Jr. was told that he had won. He was then thirty-five years old. He was the youngest man and the second African American to win the honor. In December he and Coretta went to Norway to accept the prize.

After the Kings returned home, Dr. King began a new fight. Before a person can vote, his or her name has to be on a list or register. Most black people in the South could not get their names on the list. There were many unfair rules. Dr. King tried to get black people onto the list

Dr. King in front of the Alabama state capitol building at the end of the Selma march.

in Alabama. The state leaders wouldn't allow it. Dr. King planned a fifty-four mile march. The march would start in Selma, Alabama. It would end at the state capitol building in Montgomery.

On March 6, 1965, the march began. Many white people from the North joined the Selma march. Some marchers were beaten and put into jail. Some were killed. President Lyndon Johnson ordered soldiers to protect them. Finally, 300 people reached Montgomery. Partly because of the Selma march, President Johnson asked Congress to pass a voting rights bill. In August 1965, the law was passed. Millions of black people could vote at last.

Dr. King's Death

Now Dr. King turned his attention to poor people. He held marches in Chicago, Illinois, for better housing. He planned a Poor People's March for Washington, D.C. In April 1968, he flew to Memphis, Tennessee, to help the garbage workers get equal pay.

At 6:40 P.M. on April 4, Dr. King stepped out of his hotel room. From across the street, James Earl Ray fired a shot. Dr. King fell. An hour later he was dead. Dr. Martin Luther King, Jr. was only thirty-nine years old. The world was in shock.

Dr. King was buried in Atlanta. An old farm wagon carried his body. It was pulled by two mules. Behind the wagon walked 100,000 people—rich and poor, known and unknown, black and white. On his grave are printed the words that he used to end many of his speeches, "Free at last. Free at last. Thank God Almighty, I'm free at last."

Martin Luther King, Jr. is buried in Atlanta, Georgia.

Martin Luther King, Jr. Day
Becomes a Holiday

After Dr. King's death, many people wanted to have a holiday to honor him. It had to be voted on by Congress. Every year the idea was presented. Each time there were not enough votes. But Coretta Scott King and others never gave up hope. They spoke to leaders in government. Thousands of people wrote letters. African Americans in all fifty states asked their state leaders for a holiday. On January 15, 1981, 100,000 people marched in Washington, D.C. They wanted to show how important the holiday was to them.

Finally, fifteen years after Dr. King's death, Congress voted for the holiday. On November 2, 1983, President Ronald Reagan signed the law. The third Monday of January would become Martin Luther King, Jr. Day.

Dr. King at the Lincoln Memorial in 1963. After his death, people wanted to remember Dr. King with a holiday in his honor.

Dr. King Is Remembered

A year after Dr. King's death Coretta Scott King formed the Martin Luther King, Jr. Center for Nonviolent Social Change. The center is in Atlanta. It is a way of remembering Dr. King. Dr. King is buried there. At the center, people learn about nonviolence. They come from all over the world. They read Dr. King's papers. They are taught how to use peaceful ways to change unfair laws.

Dr. King is remembered in many other ways, too. All across the country, schools, libraries, parks, and streets are named after him. In Los Angeles there is the Martin Luther King, Jr. Hospital. The Dr. Martin Luther King Bridge crosses the Mississippi River in St. Louis. The

Martin Luther King Memorial Library is in Washington, D.C. In Memphis there is a park named for him. In the country of Israel, a forest was planted to honor him. And around the world there have been over 105 different postage stamps in his honor.

The Martin Luther King Memorial Library in Washington, D.C. It is one of the ways people have honored Dr. King.

This girl is drawing a picture of Martin Luther King, Jr.

Preparing for the Holiday

Every January children prepare for Martin Luther King, Jr. Day. They read books about Dr. King. They learn about his childhood. They talk about segregation. Boys and girls draw pictures of Dr. King. They put on plays about his life.

Children talk about how to settle fights peacefully. They ask themselves, "What would Dr. King do? What would he say?" Everyone shares ideas about love instead of hate.

Some boys and girls plant trees on Dr. King's birthday. Others raise money. They might have a bake sale or sell candy. The money is given to the King Center to honor Dr. King. This helps the King Center spread Dr. King's ideas.

Films about Dr. King's life are shown. Reports are given about Dr. King's speeches. People talk about how Dr. King fought to help poor people. Children bring food and clothes to school. These are given to poor people in their neighborhood.

Everywhere, children talk about the unfair laws that Dr. King helped change. They learn why we honor this man.

The Third Monday in January

Martin Luther King, Jr. Day is a national holiday. On that day, mail is not delivered. All U.S. government offices and most banks are closed. Many schools and businesses are closed. Flags are flown everywhere. Parades are held in cities all over our country. In churches people pray for freedom. They pray that people everywhere will have fair laws.

In Atlanta and Montgomery, people visit the places where Dr. King worked and lived. Leaders of the SCLC and African-American groups give speeches about Dr. King and his dreams.

Martin Luther King, Jr. died before his dreams could come true. But his dreams live on. His words still speak to us. And on this holiday, we can remember this man who changed our country and our world.

Martin Luther King, Jr., the man whose great work we honor the third Monday in January.

Glossary

---

boycott—To join with others in refusing to deal with a person, business, or government.

capitol—A building where laws are made for a nation or state.

Civil War—The war between the northern states and the southern states from 1861 to 1865.

Congress—A branch of government that makes laws.

minister—A teacher of religion; a preacher.

Nobel Peace Prize—A prize given each year by the country of Norway to the person who has done the most that year for peace.

nonviolent—Not violent, peaceful.

president—The leader of a country or group.

resistance—The effort of fighting against or overcoming.

register—A written list or record.

segregation—The setting apart of one racial group from another racial group.

students—People who attend school.

slave—A person who is owned by another person.

Southern Christian Leadership Conference (SCLC)—A certain group formed to fight unfair laws.

Supreme Court—The highest court in the United States.

violence—Acts that hurt or destroy people, places, or things.

Index